Affirming Her

Over One Hundred Affirmations and Prayers for

Becoming the Woman You're Meant to Be

By: Jaylin Gibson

Printed in China

ISBN: 979-8-9937322-4-4

For every woman who needed a reminder of her light.

Acknowledgments

Thank you to everyone who believed in me, encouraged me, and inspired this book. This project wouldn't exist without your love and support.

To my family — thank you for always standing by me. Mom and Dad, Janice Harper and Dwight Gibson, your support has meant everything.

To my friends Orion, Tamera, and Amber, and to my God-sister Kirsten — thank you for always being there and helping me through.

To my new friends on this "becoming her" journey in Bali — Moon and Ronja — I'll never forget you.

To the late Frank Richelieu — your work deeply inspired this book. Your teachings reminded me to focus on God as our true source, and they helped shape the heart of these affirmations.

And most of all, I could not have done this without the strength and encouragement of God.

Author's Note

Writing this book has been a journey of reflection, healing, and hope. These affirmations were born in moments when I needed them most.

My prayer is that they serve you in the same way — as gentle reminders of your strength, your worth, and your beauty.

I dedicate this book to women everywhere. I know how easy it is to feel lost, overwhelmed, or unsure. But there is so much power in your words — and in your faith.

At first, I questioned whether I was the right person to write something like this. I'm young and still growing into the woman I'm becoming. But that's exactly why I chose to write it. I want to help other women

— no matter where you are in life or what your past looks like — to believe in your power to grow, to change, and to heal.

God is our source. And no matter what habits you're breaking or what life you've lived before, He is always ready to give you the strength to become the woman you're meant to be.

You deserve to meet that version of yourself.

So, as a young woman in her twenties — not perfect, not fully "qualified," but full of faith — I'm sharing the words and prayers that have helped me. May they help you too. XOXO. Jaylin

This is more than a book.

It's a mirror, a love letter, and a safe space.

Each affirmation was written to lift you when you're low, ground you when you're overwhelmed, and center you when you feel scattered. You can flip to any page or read it cover to cover — trust that what you need will find you when you need it most.

Remember to *affirm* your life — speak to who you are becoming, not just who you've been.

Live life beautifully, boldly, and with faith.

TABLE OF CONTENTS

SECTION 1: SOFTY ALIGNED

I Am Resting in Sacred Wholeness

A Prayer for the Girl Ready to Let Go and Heal

I let my guard down today.
I don't need to force or figure it all out.
There is peace moving through me now — steady, soft, and strong.

This is God within me —
quiet strength that heals and restores. Old fears melt. Heavy thoughts lift.
Tension fades. My heart opens. My spirit lightens.

I am held. I am safe. I am guided.
There is no struggle — only the peace of remembering who I am.

Nothing holds me back — not my fear, not my past, not my story.
I am aligned. I am whole.
Surely goodness and mercy are with me now — and always.

I live in love. I live in truth. I rest in sacred wholeness.

Amen,

Flowing in Grace

I give myself permission to move slower, breathe deeper, and trust the process. Everything I've prayed for is already in motion, flowing toward me in divine order. I no longer live in a state of proving or pushing. I flow — with pcacc in my heart and purpose in my steps. I attract opportunities that feel right for me, people who see the real me, and moments that nourish my spirit. I am surrounded by ease, love, and light. My life feels lighter when I let God lead.

I give myself permission to move slower, breathe deeper, and trust the process. Everything I've prayed for is already in motion, flowing toward me in divine order. I no longer live in a state of proving or pushing. I flow — with peace in my heart and purpose in my steps. I attract opportunities that feel right for me, people who see the real me, and moments that nourish my spirit. I am surrounded by ease, love, and light. My life feels lighter when I let God lead.

I See Myself Through Love's Eyes

A Prayer for the Girl Who's Learning to Love Herself Fully Soft, radiant, and complete.

I am not broken. I am not behind.

I am not missing anything.

There is a sacred light within me —placed there by the One who made me.

That light is steady. That light is enough. That light is me.

I don't have to chase worth or strive for love.

I am already held, already guided, already chosen.

When I look at myself now, I see truth: Joy in my heart.

Strength in my body. Peace in my mind. Glow in my soul.

No outside voice can cancel what God has spoken.

No reflection can distort what's eternal.

I am covered. I am centered.

I am deeply loved.

Nothing is missing. Nothing is lacking.

Every part of me is held in God's goodness.

I trust rest, and celebrate in that.

Love surrounds me.Peace flows through me.

Wholeness lives in every breath I take. This is who I am.This is how I live.

Thank you, God.

Amen.

I Am Healed, I Am Held

An affirmative prayer for peace, renewal, and divine alignment

Even when things stretch me, I stay rooted in peace. I don't run from the process — I rise within it. Every breath reminds me that God's hand is on me, guiding me, healing me, holding me steady.

I release tension and fear. I rest in faith. I know that peace is my portion. I am surrounded by divine presence and filled with holy confidence.

The Spirit of Christ is alive in me now — aligning my thoughts, renewing my energy, and restoring my body. Every cell in me vibrates with life, love, and light.

I am not waiting for healing — I *am* healing in motion. God's power flows through me effortlessly, bringing harmony to everything that concerns me.

I trust the process because I trust the Source. God is within me, and I am within God. We are one — inseparable, unstoppable, unbreakable.

Love restores everything I thought I lost. Peace fills every space that once felt uncertain. Joy rises where heaviness once lived.

I am whole. I am radiant. I am aligned with divine perfection.

The same power that created galaxies moves through me now — guiding, strengthening, and elevating me.

I don't shrink, I shine. I don't worry, I worship. I don't force, I flow.

God's love expresses through me — beautifully, boldly, and beyond limits.

I am healed. I am held. I am becoming everything I was created to be.

Amen.

Glow in the Flow

I am glowing in every season because I no longer resist the shifts. I trust that what's leaving is making space for something softer, something greater. I'm not behind — I'm being positioned. I'm not lost — I'm being guided. My energy speaks peace, my presence carries grace, and my life radiates divine alignment. I attract what feels like home, what feels like joy, and what feels like God. Everything that's meant for me recognizes my peace and flows my way naturally.

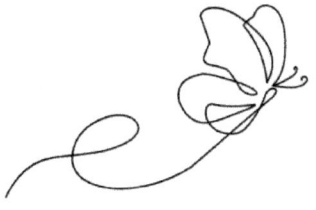

I Am Open to Gentle, Restorative Healing

A Prayer for the Girl Learning to Receive Without Resistance

I am open. I receive.

Healing is already at work within me.

The Spirit of God lives in me — and I live in that presence.

Divine life flows through every part of me.

My body feels alive. My heart feels light. My soul feels safe.

I don't need to strive. I don't need to fix.

I simply breathe and allow.

God's love moves through me now — calming my thoughts,

lifting my body, restoring my spirit.

I feel wholeness rising gently.

Here and now. Thank You, God.

I trust.

I release. I receive.

Amen.

Radiance and Wellness Flow from Me

A Prayer for the Girl Aligned with Her Body and Spirit

My body is a sacred home — a living space for the Divine.

Within me, a wise and loving power is always at work, bringing everything into balance.

Every cell, every nerve, every system knows what to do.

God's design is flawless.

And I trust that design within me. My body moves in perfect rhythm.

No stress. No struggle.

Just ease. Just grace.

Divine love is restoring me — softly, fully, completely.

I affirm flow in every part of me: circulation, digestion, release — all working in harmony with Spirit. Today, I speak truth over myself:

I am the health of God. My thoughts are kind. My feelings are light. My actions reflect love.

I radiate peace. I shine with calm.

I feel safe in my body. Grateful for its wisdom.

Healing is already happening — and I give thanks for it now.

God is here.

I trust.

I release.

I let go with joy.

Amen.

Soft Healing Clears What No Longer Belongs

A Prayer for the Girl Letting Go With Grace

The words I speak now are filled with love. They're a soft reminder: I was created whole. The same power that made me is healing me — not through force, but through love.

Quietly. Intentionally. For my highest good.

My body listens to divine order.

My spirit leans into peace.

There is no chaos here — only calm.

Whatever doesn't belong — fear, tension, worry — is being gently released.

God's presence moves through me with grace and ease.

I see myself as God sees me: Whole. Radiant. Strong. Beautiful.

I give no power to fear.

I release the things I once held onto in fear.

They are fading now.

Love is louder.

As Spirit rises in me, peace replaces the pressure.

What needs healing is healing. What needs to leave is leaving.

God's love is making all things right. This moment is a shift —
and I feel it.

I trust it.

I receive it.

Thank You, God, for the soft healing that never leaves me.

I let go. I allow.

I receive.

Amen.

Divine Energy Moves Through Me with Grace

A Prayer for the Girl Remembering Who She Is

The words I speak now are soft, but they hold power.

They remind me of what's always been true: God lives in me.

Moves through me. Expresses as me. Loves through me.

I am the life of God in motion.

I always have been.

I always will be.

There's a sacred energy flowing through every part of me — The
energy of peace, healing, and perfect health.

No fear, no doubt, no old story can undo who I really am.

I am safe in the truth. I am held by love.

Right now, God's healing power moves through me — Filling
every space.

Calming every thought. Restoring every cell.

I was made in God's image — Whole. Beautiful. Deeply loved.
So I have every right to heal.

Every right to feel joy.

Every right to live with peace and confidence.

Today, I own that truth:

I am a living expression of divine love.

I am guided.

I am supported. This is who I am. And I am grateful.

Amen.

Unconditional Love Is Gently Restoring Me

A Prayer for the Girl Learning to Trust the Timing

God sees me as whole — radiant and complete.

The same love that paints the sunrise flows through me now,

guiding my life with grace.

I don't need to rush what's already aligned.

Everything within me is unfolding in divine rhythm.

My body is sacred — a living reflection of love.

Every breath, every heartbeat, moves with purpose.

Where there was tension, peace is settling in.

God's presence flows through me, clearing out what no longer

belongs.

I am restored — in mind, in body, in spirit. Love is renewing me

from the inside out.

Each day, I wake up stronger.

Softer.

More alive.

I honor the divine order shaping my path.

I am guided.

I am supported.

I am whole.

My healing is already complete in Spirit. Everything is working for my highest good.

With peace in my heart and gratitude in my soul, I release.

I allow. I let it be.

Amen.

I Am Held in Love That Never Leaves

A Prayer for the Girl Rooted in God's Presence

Right now, I'm fully present.

Every part of me is surrounded by love.

God is not far away.

God is the steady presence within me — always here, always loving, always enough.

I am made of love. I am held by love.

I am sustained through love.

This love is healing me from the inside out.

Where love lives, fear fades.

What doesn't align with love has no space in me anymore.

God's love is working in every detail of my life — softening, restoring, transforming.

My thoughts are rooted in love. My energy is shaped by love.

The way I see the world is filtered through love.

Today, I choose to love the God within me.

This light, this truth, this peace — it lives inside me now.

And I recognize that same light in others.

Divine love is healing me now.

It always has. It always will.

Everything I need is already on its way.

Thank You, God.

I receive. I trust.

I let go and allow love to lead.

Amen.

Softly Aligned

I am in perfect rhythm with my life. Everything that's meant for me flows in divine timing — not rushed, not delayed, but beautifully on time. I no longer chase what's already aligned; I simply open my hands and receive. My peace is my power. My softness is my strength.

I move through my days with ease, trusting that God is guiding every detail. I am becoming more grounded, more graceful, and more certain of who I am. I let life unfold naturally, knowing that alignment is not something I find — it's something I allow.

SECTION 2: THE RETURN TO RADIANT WHOLENESS

I Return to Wholeness

A Prayer for the Woman Reclaiming Herself

Today, I thank God for my health — not just the kind that can be seen, but the kind that begins within: peace in my spirit, calm in my mind, and balance in my body.

This gratitude opens the door for healing to flow freely through me. The Spirit of God lives within me — whole, wise, and steady. She is not distant from me; She is my center, my truth, my peace.

In Her, I am already whole. I'm not waiting to be fixed — I'm awakening to who I've always been.

Every belief that said I wasn't enough — I release it now. Every fear that made me shrink — I let it go. I don't carry shame. I don't carry doubt.

I speak life over my body. I speak peace over my mind. I speak love over my past, my present, and my unfolding future.

The wisdom of the Creator flows through every part of me. My body is sacred. My energy is vibrant. My beauty is real — because it's grounded in truth.

The divine spark within me is rising. It fuels my healing. It fuels my softness. It fuels my strength.

I honor this version of me. I honor my process, even when it feels uncertain. I honor myself — not because I'm perfect, but because I was created with intention and love.

Amen.

And so it is.

Healing Is Happening Now

A Prayer for the Woman Trusting Her Restoration

God is here — in this breath, in this moment, in every part of me. She is not distant. She is within me, moving, restoring, guiding.

The Spirit that holds the universe together also holds me.

Alive. Active. Present.

I don't chase healing — I claim it.

I declare that restoration is already happening in my body, in my mind, and in my heart.

God's power doesn't delay.

It works in divine timing — and that timing is now.

I let go of every lie that told me I was broken or too far gone.

That story is over. I am not behind.

I am not incomplete.

I am being renewed in real time.

Where there was pain, peace settles in. Where fear used to speak, faith takes over.

Where doubt once lived, I plant new seeds of truth.

The power of God lives in me — and I trust that power fully.

It flows through my thoughts. It moves through my words. It shapes my every step.

My body knows how to heal. My mind knows how to rest. My spirit knows how to rise. I align with that knowing.

I align with divine intelligence. I align with life, love, and light.

Right here, right now — not one day, not "when I'm better" — I affirm this truth:

Healing is here. God is here. And I am whole.

Amen.

I Receive My Healing with Joy and Trust

A Prayer for the Woman Learning to Receive

Right here, right now — I know that God is with me.

Not far off, not waiting — present, loving, and alive within.

Divine wisdom moves through my thoughts.

Pure love strengthens my spirit.

The creative force of God breathes life into every part of who I
am.

I am open. I am willing.

I am ready to receive.

Right now, God's healing power flows through me — Gently,
fully, and without delay.

My body is responding. My mind is clearing. My spirit is rising.

I don't need to chase healing — I allow it. I don't need to earn
peace — I say yes to it.

What God has for me doesn't require force — only faith.

With joy, I say yes to clarity.

Yes to alignment. Yes to peace.

Yes to my full restoration.

The light of Christ is working in me right now — Not someday, not when I "get it all together." Now.

My healing is here.

In my body. In my mind.

In my relationships.

In the quiet spaces no one sees.

I don't wait for a sign.

I speak it in faith:

I accept my healing. I trust my wholeness.

And I let love finish what it started in me.

Amen.

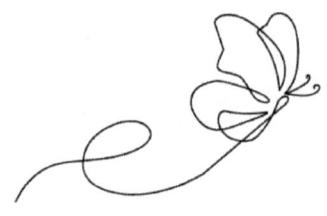

Radiant Renewal

I am glowing from the inside out — healed, whole, and held by divine love.

What once hurt me has become my strength, what once dimmed me now refines my light.

Every part of me radiates peace, beauty, and power because I chose to rise gently.

My healing is not hidden — it shines through my smile, my confidence, and my calm.

I am proof that strength can be soft, and healing can be radiant.

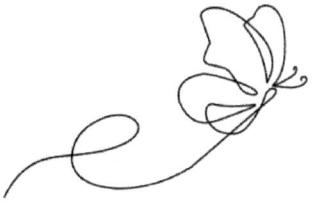

Divine Strength Flows Through My Body and Soul

A Prayer for the Woman Remembering Her Power

There is a steady strength inside me — Not loud, not forced —
just real.

It lives in the quiet center of who I am,

Where God breathes, moves, and reminds me: I am not alone.

I wasn't created to struggle — I was created to remember.

To remember that I'm loved.

To remember that I'm supported.

To remember that everything I need is already within.

So today, I release the noise.

The pressure. The proving. The performance.

I breathe deeply.

I soften. I listen.

Be still, my heart. Be still, my mind.

There is nothing to chase, and nothing to fear. The same Presence that created me sustains me.

When I feel unsure, I return inward —

To the truth, to the calm, to the Spirit that knows.

Divine wisdom rises.Divine timing unfolds.

Divine order holds me, even when I can't see the full picture.

I trust the quiet.I trust the timing.

I trust the sacred rhythm that's guiding my life.

Today, I move in faith, not force. I create from fullness, not fear.

I lead with peace, not pressure.

This is my truth:

I am steady.I am whole.

I am held.

And I am ready.

Amen.

Grace Made Me Strong

I'm walking in joy, covered in grace, and glowing from the inside out. This season of my life feels light, full, and aligned — because I finally let go and let God.

My heart is open, my spirit is steady, and everything around me reflects the peace within me.

I don't carry the weight of the past — I carry wisdom, laughter, and gratitude.

Every day, I wake up feeling more like myself: confident, radiant, and deeply favored.

I'm not just healed — I'm whole. I'm not just surviving — I'm soaring.

And the glow? That's all God.

A Higher Power Moves Through Me

A Prayer for the Woman Trusting Her Inner Restoration

There is a sacred power moving in me now — Gentle, steady,
and alive.

It's the breath of Spirit. The heartbeat of God.

The quiet current that flows through every part of who I am.

I am never alone.

I am held by a Love that's greater than anything I can see.

Right now, divine balance is settling into my thoughts, my body,
and my spirit.

Anything that no longer belongs — I release it.

Old weight falls away. Fear loses its grip.

This moment becomes enough. This moment becomes holy.

I stop reaching. I stop resisting.

I soften.

I let the presence of God do what only grace can do.

Restore me. Renew me. Reveal me. Truth rises. Wisdom flows.

Love holds it all together.

Everything in me that isn't aligned with God's peace dissolves.

Not because I forced it — but because I allowed it.

Healing is not a chase — it's a surrender.

And I surrender now. With open hands. With an open heart. With deep gratitude.

I say yes.

Yes to peace. Yes to grace.

Yes to the power that's healing me now.

Amen

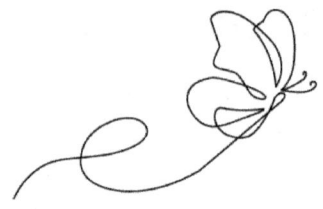

Healing Looks Good on Me

My heart is healing in divine order. What once broke me is now building me.

Every tear watered the garden of my glow — and I see new beauty rising from where pain once lived.

I release the story that hurt me, and I return to the peace that holds me. Love didn't leave; it transformed. It lives within me now — softer, wiser, stronger.

I no longer chase closure; I embody it.

God is rewriting this chapter with gentleness and grace, and I trust that what's meant for me will always find its way back in love.

I am healing. I am radiant. I am becoming whole again — beautifully, softly, completely.

My Focus Calls in Full-Body Wholeness

A Prayer for the Woman Who Sees With Spiritual Eyes

I don't need to chase clarity — it lives in me. When I quiet the
noise, I hear what matters. God is here. Steady. Close. Always
enough.

I am not broken. I am not behind.
I don't need to earn my wholeness — I was born with it.

The pressure to prove, to fix, to force — I release it.
I trust the process. I trust the timing.
I trust the truth that never changes.

Healing isn't a future goal. It's a present choice.
And I choose it now.

I see with faith. I walk with peace.
I align with love.

No more striving. No more shrinking.
Just me — grounded, glowing, guided.

Amen.

I Am Radiantly Whole, Complete and Enough

A Prayer for the Girl Walking in Her Worth

Today, I rise with intention.

This body—strong, beautiful, and sacred—carries the presence of
something greater.

Each step I take is guided.

Each breath reminds me I'm alive for a reason.

I welcome clarity into my mind.

I open to wisdom that flows through my thoughts, my choices,
and my spirit.

I don't chase alignment — I create it. What I need to know
becomes clear.

There is divine order in my life, even when I don't see it all yet.

I'm not stuck — I'm becoming.

Health flows through me like rhythm.

Solutions don't arrive through force — they come through faith.

I recognize what feels right. I follow what brings peace.

Within me, a calm strength rises. Not loud, not rushed — but real.

I honor the quiet knowing inside me.

I trust it to guide me where hype never could.

Today isn't just another day — It's mine.

And I move through it with grace, power, and full awareness of who I am.

I am whole. I am enough. I am already becoming her.

Amen.

The Power That Heals Is Always by My Side

A Prayer for the Girl Who's Learning to Trust the Process

There's something unfolding in me —
and even if I can't see the full picture yet, I know it's good.
I'm not behind. I'm not broken. I'm becoming.
Every moment is shaping me gently, quietly, on purpose.

I don't have to rush the process. I don't have to force the
outcome.
What's meant for me is already moving toward me — guided by
grace, not pressure.

I was made by a God who sees the big picture.
And that same wisdom lives in me —
in my breath, in my choices, in the quiet knowing that keeps me
steady.

So today, I release the need to control, compare, or question my pace.

I don't chase timelines. I don't cling to doubt.

I choose trust —

Not someday, not when it's all perfect, but right now.

I honor this season.

I celebrate small steps.

I speak gently to myself, because I know: growth is still growth,

even when it's silent.

And when it's time, everything will align — not because I

pushed,

but because I trusted.

Amen.

Every Cell in Me Is Cleansed, Restored, and Renewed

A Prayer for the Girl Releasing and Restoring

My body is sacred — created with care, designed with love.

It carries divine wisdom, and I treat it with honor.

I don't need perfection. I need presence.

Today, I choose to cleanse what no longer serves me.

Old energy. Past stories. Heavy emotions.

I let them go with peace and intention.

Order flows through me now — In my mind, in my body, in my spirit.

God's healing power is already at work, Restoring what's been drained, Renewing what's been forgotten.

I don't fight for healing — I align with it.

I speak life over myself.

I choose thoughts that bring peace.

I release anything that blocks my wholeness.

Right now, I return to balance.

I trust the divine rhythm flowing within me.

I am clear. I am grounded.

I am restored by the One who made me.

Amen.

Living on Purpose

SECTION 3: PURPOSE IN MOTION, SPIRIT IN FLOW

I Walk a Path of Purpose and Progress

A Prayer for the Girl Trusting the Flow

I am on a gentle journey of becoming.

With every step, I open to more beauty, more grace, more light.

The presence of God surrounds me and fills me — renewing my mind,

restoring my spirit, refreshing my body with ease.

Divine wisdom flows from within.

It leads me softly, clearly, and always toward purpose.

Wherever I go, God is already there.

There is no space without love.

This truth grounds me.

This truth lifts me.

Every decision is supported. Every move is met with grace.

Creative ideas rise easily in me, shaping a life I love.

I don't need to fight or force.

What looks like a block fades in the light of truth.

God is my quiet strength — my calm confidence, my steady shield.

I am wrapped in divine protection.

I am guarded by love. I am guided in peace.

I move forward gracefully — no rush, no pressure, only flow.

In every area of my life, success unfolds gently.

Life loves me. Life supports me. And I receive it fully.

I walk in peace. I walk in trust.

I walk in purpose.

Amen

Spiritual Awareness Fuels My Energy

A Prayer for the Girl Who Moves With Alignment, Not Pressure

I live in the flow of divine energy.

Life moves through me — steady, strong, and light. Every part of me is lifted by the presence of God.

I stay energized not by doing more, but by staying in tune with what's true.

My spirit is light.

My body is at peace. My life flows with ease.

I don't need to push to prove.

My peace is my power.

My confidence comes from the Source that holds me.

I move through life open and soft — trusting the rhythm, trusting the plan.

I release fear.

I release control.

I let good things come to me with ease.

I don't cling. I don't chase.

I give to what aligns. I pour into what's true.

And what I give comes back multiplied.

God is the wellspring of all energy.

I am fully connected.

There is no burnout in Spirit —

only steady strength, pure joy, and divine flow.

Everything good is available to me.

Not because I force, but because I align.

I move forward with grace.

I rise in peace. I live in trust.

Walking in Purpose

I am walking in divine purpose, guided by a wisdom that never fails me. Each step I take is intentional, even when the path feels uncertain. I trust that God is aligning my journey with grace — clearing what's not for me and blessing what is. Purpose doesn't demand perfection; it asks for faith. I am learning that obedience and peace are stronger than fear or doubt. Even when I can't see the full picture, I know I'm part of something greater unfolding. I walk with my head high and my heart open, knowing that every detour, delay, and decision is preparing me for destiny. My life is a reflection of divine order — purposeful, powerful, and full of promise.

I Co-Create My Life with God

A Prayer for the Girl Who's Ready to Flow, Not Force

Today, I step into a new awareness.

I open my heart to fresh thoughts, softer energy, and more peace.

I release the pressure. I let go of the heaviness.

I choose joy. I choose ease. I choose flow.

I don't have to hustle to grow — I just need to align.

Love transforms me from the inside out.

I walk differently now. I speak from truth.

I move with calm intention.

I see myself the way God sees me — Full of purpose, full of grace, fully enough.

I was created on purpose, in love.

I belong here.

There's a rhythm, a plan, a path — and I'm already on it.

I stop fighting the current.

I float in faith.

I stop forcing outcomes.

I expect goodness.

I expect joy.

I expect beauty.

My connection with God is my confidence.

I'm not alone.

I'm not meant to figure it all out alone.

God is my partner in this life — and with Him beside me, I move boldly. I meet today with softness, with strength, and with trust in every step.

Amen.

My Life Overflows with Spiritual Richness

A Prayer for the Girl Who Leads with Peace, Not Pressure

I lead my life with peace.

Not force. Not fear.

Just steady trust in the One who walks with me.

God guides. I listen.

And together, we build something beautiful.

I'm gentle with my thoughts, kind with my choices.

If it doesn't protect my peace, I lovingly release it.

My inner world creates my outer world — so I choose calm.

I choose joy. I choose faith.

Every day brings a choice — and today, I choose alignment.

I choose to trust the rhythm God designed for me.

I plan with ease.

I move with purpose.

Whatever shows up, I know I'm ready — because I am guided.

I am supported. I am equipped.

I carry joy. I walk softly.

I decide with wisdom and love.

My life is full because I let love lead.

I welcome creativity, clarity, and divine surprises.

This day is new.

This path is blessed. And I walk it with grace. God is my compass.

Peace is my direction.

I'm not striving. I'm aligned.

Amen.

Progress Over Perfection

I no longer rush my growth or force my timing. I understand that becoming her — the woman I'm meant to be — is a journey, not a race. Every lesson, every pause, every redirection is part of the beauty of progress. I give myself grace to evolve, to outgrow, to rest, and to rise again. Perfection no longer defines me — peace does. I celebrate how far I've come and trust that what's ahead will meet me with favor. I am proud of my becoming, even in the middle of the process. I am learning to love my story as it unfolds — softly, steadily, and in divine order.

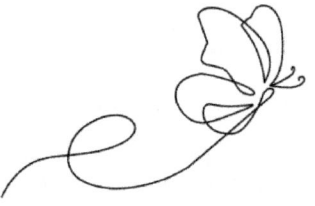

My Spirit Is a Source of True Wealth

A Prayer for the Girl Aligned with Inner Abundance

I am rich in spirit.

My wealth starts within — in love, in peace, in grace.

The more I rest in God's goodness, the more it shows up in my life.

I move through my day with quiet confidence.

Not chasing. Not forcing. Just aligned. Just full.

Whatever I do, I do with joy.

I lead my life from a place of peace.

My thoughts are steady.

My heart is full.

My steps are intentional.

I find beauty in the little things.

In the work. In the growth. In the rest. I don't wait for joy — I live it now.

My happiness doesn't depend on outcomes.

It comes from knowing I'm loved, guided, and blessed.

I breathe in peace. I exhale gratitude.

I attract good things because I live in harmony with them.

Success isn't something I chase.

It's what naturally flows from faith, focus, and calm.

I stay open to fresh ideas, new beauty, and divine opportunities.

I trust life's timing.

I move with grace and ease. Abundance is my birthright — and I see it everywhere:

In how I love. In how I live. In how I shine.

Amen.

I Am Rising Into My Divine Timing

A Prayer for the Girl Trusting Her Season

I belong to life — the one God designed with love and intention.

This is my time. My season. My story.

And I choose to live it fully.

Right now, I show up with gratitude and presence.

I connect with myself, with my emotions, with what's real.

Every feeling I honor opens a door — to healing, to creativity, to growth.

I stay open to what's good and new.

I welcome experiences that align with peace.

My thoughts, energy, and actions are all moving me forward — toward the best version of me.

I am whole.

I am complete. Nothing is missing.

Everything I need is already within. God awakens my potential day by day. And I rise into it softly, faithfully, in flow.

Even when things feel uncertain, I know I'm being shaped.

Every challenge is a chance to expand.

To love deeper. To trust more. To become.

I am an unfolding masterpiece — growing at the pace of grace.

Today, I choose joy.

I choose love.

I choose this life — fully. The past has passed.

I walk forward free. This moment is holy. This day is blessed.

And I belong here, exactly as I am. This is the day the Lord has made — and I receive it with an open heart.

Amen.

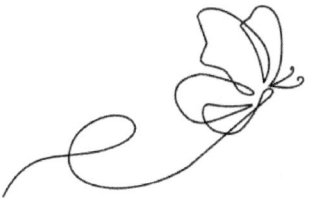

My Greatest Good Begins Within Me

A Prayer for the Girl Growing at God's Pace

Today, I move with grace —

in rhythm with what God has set for me.

I don't rush. I don't force.

I trust divine timing, knowing I'm guided by love.

I believe in the power God placed in me — soft, steady, and
strong.

His Spirit gives me courage, grace to grow, and peace to rest.

Life is unfolding in my favor —not because I chase it, but
because I'm aligned with Him.

God sustains me, uplifts me, and expands me into clarity.

My highest good isn't far —it's here, within me,

working around me.

I'm called to live fully, love deeply, and shine with purpose.

As I rise, so does everything connected to me.

My peace. My health. My vision.

I don't just receive good things —I carry them.

Right now, His love renews me.

My heart is calm. My mind is clear. My spirit is at peace.

Thank You, God, for this becoming.

Amen.

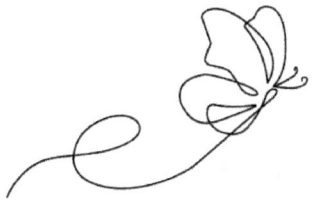

I Am Built to Thrive and Succeed

A Prayer for the Girl Who's Growing with God

I begin this day with a thankful heart.

Before I take a step, I honor the One who ordered my steps. God has already prepared blessings and opportunities for me — and I receive them with joy.

What I hold in faith, I will see in my life.

When I speak from "I am,"

I connect to who God created me to be.

And from that truth, "I have" begins to unfold.

My life is an expression of God's life — growing, progressing, becoming.

I'm not racing.

I'm in rhythm with His will.

Each day, I grow softer in spirit, stronger in faith,

clearer in purpose.

There are no limits on what God can do through me.

No ceilings on what He can release in my life.

Today, I take aligned action — gentle, intentional, and led by peace.

I listen closely to His guidance. I honor the ideas He gives me.

And I trust what flows from love and light.

As I move forward, I expand.

My mind stays open. My heart stays light.

My soul stays refreshed.

God's presence fills every part of me — restoring, inspiring, and making me whole.

Today, I walk in purpose.

I move with grace. I live in gratitude.

I am progressing in love.

I am thriving in faith.

I am blooming in God's care.

Amen.

Built to Thrive

I was never created to shrink, settle, or survive — I was built to thrive. Everything about me — my mind, my heart, my spirit — was designed for growth and greatness. Even in challenges, I rise with resilience; even in waiting, I bloom with faith. My energy attracts abundance because I live in alignment with my purpose. I no longer question my worthiness to receive — I understand that thriving is my birthright. God didn't just create me to exist; He created me to live fully, beautifully, and boldly. My life is overflowing with good things, not by luck, but by divine design.

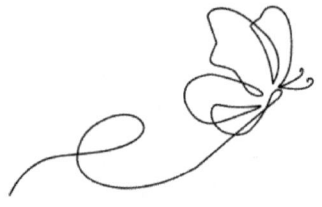

I Tap Into My Infinite Inner Power

A Prayer for the Girl Who Knows Her Strength Comes from God

I am a reflection of the Divine —

created in love, shaped by wisdom, filled with light.

Everything God is, He placed within me. His intelligence flows through my mind. His creativity moves through my heart.

His peace anchors my spirit.

There are no limits on who I can become.

I was made in the image of endless possibility.

When I move with faith and alignment, I don't have to strive — I trust.

I rise with confidence in the One who made me capable.

I don't define myself by fear or limits. I see beyond what looks possible and return to the truth:

My reality is love. My nature is peace.

My essence is wholeness.

God's Spirit is the source of all good — and I come from that source.

So goodness is in me too.

I wasn't made to question my worth.

I was made to reflect His grace, His excellence,

and His quiet strength.

Every dream I carry

is connected to God's plan for me.

Every step I take in love moves me deeper into His will.

My potential is endless. My path is wide open.

And I'm walking it in peace.

I can do what I'm called to do. I can be all He created me to be.

God sustains me. God empowers me.

God loves me — fully and forever.

I am guided by love.

I am strengthened by peace.

I am upheld by grace.

Amen.

My Work Is a Sacred Extension of My Purpose

A Prayer for the Girl Who Creates From a Place of Peace

There is one divine Mind — the mind of God — and I am fully connected to it.

My thoughts are clear.

My heart is calm. My spirit is led.

Every idea I need arrives right on time.

I don't second-guess my path. I move with quiet confidence,

trusting that the same wisdom that shaped the stars is guiding my steps.

God's intelligence lives in me — shaping my choices, directing my thoughts, anchoring me in peace.

I welcome divine ideas.

I speak with love.

I act from alignment, not pressure.

I am a vessel —

and God's creativity flows freely through me.

My work is sacred because it's rooted in purpose.

Whatever I build, manage, or create is part of a bigger plan unfolding through me.

I don't force success. I follow divine direction.

God's life moves through me as joy, purpose, and ease.

Every part of my journey is touched by His grace.

I am guided. I am equipped.

I am exactly where I need to be.

Amen.

Love Is the Power That Moves Through Me

A Prayer for the Girl Aligned with God's Heart

Today, I choose to see with the eyes of love.

To listen with love.

To move and speak with love — because God is love, and His Spirit lives in me.

As I recognize love around me, I begin to attract it in all forms — kind people, peaceful moments, divine opportunities.

Even in uncertainty, I look deeper and find God's love holding it all together.

Every person I meet is a chance to reflect love. Every task I touch is a chance to move with grace.

I don't need to strive to be enough — I already am.

Because when I show up in love, I bring value to every space I enter.

My work flows from joy, not pressure.

What I give comes from peace, and what I give returns to me as favor, provision, and calm.

I don't chase what's meant for me.

I welcome it.

I attract it through trust, through softness, through love.

Love removes the pressure. Love softens the process. Love multiplies the blessing.

Love is my strength. Love is my rhythm. Love is my power.

And through love — through God — I thrive.

And so it is.

Amen.

Divine Wisdom Fulfills My Every Need

A Morning Prayer for the Girl Rooted, Guided, and Renewed

I step into this day with clarity and calm strength.

I release anything that tries to dim my light or distract my focus.

What's meant for me will find me — not because I chase it,

but because I walk in alignment.

Peace is mine. Power is mine. Joy is mine.

Not from the world,

but from the One who created me.

I don't need to force. I don't need to fear.

God's provision is already written into my story.

Doors don't open by accident — they open by divine design.

I welcome clarity. I welcome favor.

I welcome the next version of me.

The Spirit within me is wise and steady.

It protects, corrects, and leads me with love.

I align my thoughts with truth: I am not behind.

I am not lacking.

I am exactly where I need to be to receive what's next.

God's grace surrounds every step I take. Even when I can't see the whole picture, I trust the path is good.

I am renewed in my thinking.

I am grounded in spirit.

I am growing in both seen and unseen ways.

Today, I move with peace.

I move with purpose. And I move in trust —

because I know I'm guided by something greater than me.

Amen.

Affirming Life Daily

I affirm life with every breath I take. I speak blessings over my days and choose joy as my default language. My words carry power — they shape the world around me, so I fill them with gratitude, faith, and expectancy. I remind myself daily that I am not behind, I am being guided. Everything is working for my good, even what I can't yet see. I am learning to live in flow with God's timing — to release control and receive peace. Life is not something happening to me; it's happening through me. I am a vessel of divine creativity, abundance, and grace. Every moment is sacred, and

every day I rise a little brighter, a little softer, a little more sure of who I am.

SECTION 4: GODFIDENCE & GLOW

Prayer for Expansion & Clarity

For the girl becoming her higher self I expand with ease.

My thoughts are no longer scattered or small.

I choose alignment over confusion. I choose clarity over chaos.

There is one Source — steady, powerful, divine. And it's not far from me — it lives within me.

I don't need to search outside of myself for truth.

Truth flows from the Spirit that lives in me.

Today, I release the idea that life has to be hard.

I don't need to struggle to be worthy.

I don't need to fight to be heard.

The same Power that shaped the stars breathes life into my dreams.

It does not resist me — it *empowers* me.

My desires are not random — they are rooted in purpose.

I'm allowed to want more.

I'm allowed to grow past who I used to be. I'm allowed to evolve, elevate, and expand. I speak life into the direction I'm heading.

My thoughts are in agreement with God's goodness.

I don't wrestle with fear — I rest in faith.

Every step I take is backed by divine strength. My confidence is not ego — it's faith in motion.

I move forward with power, because God walks with me.

Today, I expand my understanding.

I grow in wisdom. I grow in joy. I grow in grace.

And it shows in every part of my life.

Amen.

Fresh Faith, New Energy

For the woman who's done doubting and ready to decide who she's becoming

Today, I choose a new mindset — one built on faith, focus, and favor. I no longer move from fear; I move with intention. I'm releasing hesitation and stepping fully into my next level.

My thoughts are fertile ground, and every idea planted by God has purpose. I trust the divine flow of creativity within me — it's endless, inspired, and uniquely mine.

I follow through on what I start. I make bold, confident decisions that align with my highest self. I'm a magnet for peace, joy, and opportunities that match my energy.

I see myself rising — becoming more grounded, more graceful, more guided.

Every day, I'm creating a life that reflects God's goodness through me.

And that's the energy I'm keeping.

Becoming Her: Expanding in Grace

An affirmative prayer for growth, freedom, and divine purpose

God is the source of my strength, the foundation of my peace, and the power that sustains me. My life is unfolding exactly as it should, and I am open to the lessons, blessings, and new levels of awareness each season brings.

Growth feels natural to me now. I release what no longer serves me and make space for greater joy, peace, and clarity. The same energy that created me continues to expand through me

—guiding my purpose, fueling my creativity, and blessing every part of my journey.

I think and speak from a place of truth and power. My words carry life and intention, shaping my world with love and alignment.

I no longer look back in regret; I move forward in peace. Every thought, every prayer, every decision is lifting me into higher awareness.

Health, happiness, and harmony are my birthright. I walk with integrity and live with purpose. My life is expanding in divine order, and everything good is finding its way to me.

I am aligned. I am growing. I am free.

I Am in Full Bloom

I am a woman in full bloom — radiant, evolving, and grounded in divine timing. I no longer rush my becoming or compare my process to anyone else's. I trust that where I am is sacred, and what's for me will always meet me in peace. My glow is not something I chase; it's something that grows as I honor myself. I've learned to water my soul with gentleness, to prune what no longer serves me, and to bask in the light of my own becoming. Every chapter of my life — even the quiet, messy, or uncertain ones — is growing something beautiful within me. I am becoming more confident, more graceful, more rooted in love each day. My energy blooms effortlessly because I'm aligned with purpose. I am not behind. I am in season.

Becoming Her: Aligned & Anointed

Affirmations for the girl who's growing in grace, glowing in purpose, and giving God the credit

I am a reflection of God's creative brilliance — the same power that formed the galaxies flows through me. I'm not here by accident. Every season I step into is shaping me for something greater.

I welcome growth, even when it stretches me, because I know God is guiding my process. I'm learning, healing, and rising into new levels of awareness with grace and confidence.

release the past with love. I let go of anything that no longer aligns with who I'm becoming. My words carry power, and my faith makes things move.

I speak life over my dreams. I speak peace over my mind. I speak favor over my journey.

The same Spirit that lifted me before will sustain me again. My life expands in beauty, in joy, and in purpose — and God's hand is on every part of it.

And it is so.

Infinite Glow, Divine Flow

For the woman who knows her intuition is where God whispers

I am connected to divine intelligence — the same wisdom that designed the stars also moves through me. When I quiet my mind, I can feel God guiding my thoughts, aligning me with peace and purpose.

I'm open to inspired ideas that elevate my life. I release what's no longer serving me and make room for what's meant to bless me.

Every block is being cleared. Every doubt is dissolving. Nothing can stand between me and the life God is shaping for me.

I trust the answers within me, because the One who created me also lives in me. I'm guided in every decision, every moment, every move.

My spirit is in sync with divine flow — and everything I touch reflects the light I carry.

Confidence Looks Good on Me

Confidence is my quiet power — it doesn't need to shout to be seen. I carry it softly, like sunlight through sheer curtains — steady, natural, undeniable. I no longer shrink to make others comfortable, nor do I wait for validation to feel valuable. My worth is not up for debate; it's woven into my being. I move through life knowing that I am guided, equipped, and worthy of every good thing coming my way.

Confidence, for me, is peace — it's the knowing that I'm safe in my own presence. I honor my voice, I trust my vision, and I walk with the assurance that God goes before me. I wear grace like perfume — light, feminine, unforgettable. I am radiant not because everything is perfect, but because I am perfectly aligned with who I was created to be

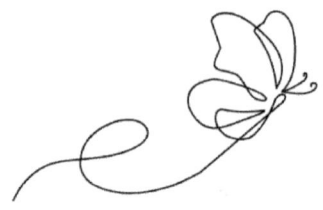

Open Hands, Overflowing Heart

For the woman who's ready to receive everything God already wrote for her

I am the living expression of divine power and purpose. God's life moves through me now — limitless, abundant, and alive.

I am aligned with everything meant for me. New ideas, divine opportunities, and unexpected blessings flow into my life with ease.

I do not chase — I attract. My energy, my faith, and my peace draw in everything that belongs to me.

My confidence is unshakable because I know my source. I am sustained by God, not by approval, titles, or things. My supply is endless because my Creator is endless.

Every door I walk through is divine. I move in perfect timing and favor follows me wherever I go. The same power that shaped the stars is shaping my story.

I live in overflow — spiritually, mentally, financially, and emotionally. Heaven is pouring blessings I am fully ready to receive.

My cup is full. My heart is open. My life is proof of what faith can manifest.

I am guided. I am provided for. I am chosen. And I am already living in the overflow.

Vision in Bloom

For the woman who knows her imagination is her anointing

God placed divine creativity within me — the ability to see beyond what is and imagine what could be. That vision is a gift, and I choose to use it with purpose.

Today, I train my thoughts to rise higher. I release worry, comparison, and fear, and I redirect that energy into faith-filled imagination. Every image I hold in my mind becomes a seed of what's possible through God's power.

I don't see challenges as setbacks; I see them as stepping stones. Every experience, even the painful ones, pushes me closer to peace, strength, and purpose.

I fill my mind with images of wholeness, abundance, love, and joy. I imagine the life God promised me and trust that He's aligning every detail.

My imagination isn't wishful thinking — it's holy vision. It's how heaven whispers ideas that manifest on earth.

I am grateful for the power to see beauty before it appears, to dream boldly, and to watch those dreams unfold.

My vision is blessed. My faith is active. My future is already forming in divine color

Crowned in Calling

For the woman walking in grace, guided by divine timing

As infinite wisdom once guided Esther — positioning her with purpose and grace — I know that same divine hand is guiding me now. God's presence goes before me, preparing the way and aligning every detail for my good.

The "I Am" within me is my anchor, my quiet confidence, and my source of strength. Like Esther, I move with discernment, knowing when to speak, when to pause, and when to stand in the fullness of who I am.

I am led by peace, not pressure. Every opportunity that is meant for me flows effortlessly into my life, and every season teaches me something about the woman I'm becoming.

God's spirit in me is both gentle and powerful — it elevates my thoughts, sharpens my vision, and fills me with courage.

I release fear and choose faith. I walk in elegance and authority, trusting that divine favor surrounds me.

I am aligned with destiny. I am prepared for my moment.

I am chosen — just like Esther.

My Glow Is Sacred

My glow is more than beauty — it's my energy, my healing, my faith made visible. I shine differently when I'm at peace with where I am and grateful for how far I've come. My glow isn't loud or forced; it's a quiet confidence that comes from knowing I'm covered, chosen, and loved by something greater. Every morning, I wake up softer — softer with myself, softer with others — and somehow, that softness makes me stronger. I am glowing because I've learned to let go, to rest, and to trust. I radiate love because I've made peace with my past and found joy in my present. My light is contagious, my presence magnetic, my spirit unbreakable. I'm not just glowing — I'm growing, expanding, and becoming the brightest version of me.

The Power Within Her

For the woman who carries God's presence in every breath

There is only one true Power — the Spirit of God — and it moves through me completely. I am aligned with that power; it fills my mind, my body, and my spirit with divine harmony.

The same presence that keeps the universe in balance is alive within me right now. Every heartbeat, every thought, every cell in my body follows divine order. Nothing about me is misplaced

— I am perfectly crafted by the Creator.

My soul is whole. My essence is pure. The woman I am becoming already exists within me — radiant, complete, and filled with purpose.

I am a reflection of God's creativity, a living masterpiece of love and light.

Everything about me — my mind, my body, my presence — carries beauty, grace, and intention. I was designed to shine, not strive.

I embrace the fullness of who I am, and I walk boldly in that truth.

God's power flows through me — steady, sacred, and strong.

She Can Because God Is With Her

For the woman who believes in herself because she believes in Him

I acknowledge the divine wisdom that lives within me and surrounds me. There's no moment of my life where God's presence isn't near — His guidance is the breath beneath my confidence.

With faith in my heart, I affirm: *I can.*

When I think *I can*, Heaven moves. Every time I believe, God aligns the pieces. There is no blockage that can stand against divine flow, no delay that can deny what's destined for me.

I release every thought of fear, lack, and limitation. I am not small, unworthy, or forgotten — I am chosen, creative, and capable.

I live in the rhythm of grace: giving and receiving, trusting and creating.

I can rise. I can rebuild. I can walk in peace, prosperity, and purpose.

God's presence within me is power — unshakable, undeniable, unstoppable.

Today, I say yes to the good waiting for me.

And I stand in the knowing: *I can, because God already did.*

SECTION 5: FAITH, FLOW & FULL

Her Mind Is a Masterpiece

An affirmative prayer for peace, joy, and divine vision

The presence of God lives in me, and I feel that love here and now.

I am surrounded by peace. I radiate joy. I move through this day with divine enthusiasm and purpose. Everything I do is touched by grace, and everything I create brings beauty into the world.

I look within and see the goodness that's already growing.

Today, I walk through the gallery of my mind and choose what stays. I replace fear with faith, worry with trust, and doubt with confidence.

My thoughts are holy ground — I fill them only with love, light, and truth.

I am intentional with every picture I paint in my mind. I see health. I see happiness. I see abundance and divine alignment. I choose joy. I choose peace. I choose God's vision for my life.

My inner world reflects His glory — and my life is the art.

Centered in Her Peace

An affirmative prayer for divine awareness, abundance, and calm

I center myself in stillness and remember who I am — a reflection of God's awareness in human form. His presence flows through me, guiding every step, every thought, every detail of my becoming.

I am fully aware that God is within me, around me, and working through me. Every answer I need comes with ease. Every opportunity meant for me finds its way to me in divine timing.

I move with grace and confidence, knowing I am supported by the same power that sustains the stars. Peace is my posture.

Faith is my foundation.

Right now, divine illumination fills my mind. I see clearly, love deeply, and act wisely. Only good can come to me, because God is the source of all that I attract.

Abundance flows effortlessly into my life — abundance of love, joy, creativity, and peace. I am aware of how blessed I truly am.

Love softens my words. Peace guards my heart. Harmony

surrounds my path.

I am immersed in the divine — whole, radiant, and beautifully aware.

And it is so.

Her Turning Point

An affirmative prayer for renewal, love, and divine strength

I am a divine expression of God's Spirit — radiant, whole, and guided. This moment marks a sacred turning point in my life.

From here forward, I move with faith, not fear.

God is my strength and my steady help in every need. His love heals every part of me — mind, body, and soul. I am overflowing with wisdom, grace, and divine presence.

I recognize God as my closest companion — walking with me, speaking through me, and sustaining me in all things.

Everything in my life is aligning for my highest good.

I am surrounded by love because I am made in the image of Love. I choose to see my life through God's eyes — filled with peace, beauty, and purpose.

Today, I begin again. I release the past with gratitude and step boldly into what God has prepared for me.

I am directed, protected, and completely sustained by divine order. My heart believes. My mind agrees. My spirit rejoices. Surely, goodness and mercy follow me — not just someday, but today and always.

I dwell in God's presence now and forever.

Flowing in Faith

I am no longer forcing what's meant to flow. I trust that what's for me will never miss me, because God's timing is always perfect. I release the need to control every outcome and instead rest in divine rhythm. My faith makes me flexible — I can bend, but I never break. I let peace lead me, knowing that I'm being guided exactly where I'm meant to go. I trust the process, I trust the pauses, and I trust that every closed door is protection, not punishment. Life moves smoothly when I move with faith, not fear. Today, I flow with grace — effortless, guided, and deeply aligned.

The Flow of Her Becoming

An affirmative prayer for expansion, faith, and divine movement

Life is always unfolding — and that same life flows through me.
I am the vessel through which God expresses creativity, beauty,
and purpose.

Today, I allow divine energy to expand through me. My soul is
open, my mind is clear, and my spirit is ready for more. I never
experience delay, because I move in rhythm with God's perfect
timing.

There is a sacred pulse within me — steady, strong, and full of
momentum. I flow with life, not against it. I am flexible, open,
and receptive to every new beginning that carries God's
goodness.

I am willing to change. I am willing to grow. I am willing to
believe that what's next holds only more love, more grace, and
more good for me.

Divine energy fills every part of my being. It moves through my thoughts, my words, and my actions. I am centered, confident, and creative.

God's Spirit lives in me — it radiates from me in every direction.

I am the temple of divine presence. I am limitless potential made real.

My life expands beautifully, gracefully, and in divine order.

And so it is.

Becoming Her, Becoming Free

An affirmative prayer for spiritual maturity, confidence, and divine identity

Today, I step into my divine maturity — fully aware of who I am and whose I am. I walk in the fullness of my spiritual inheritance, free to express the woman God created me to be.

I am no longer shaped by limitation or fear. I honor the lessons of my past — from family, culture, and experience — but I no longer let them define my truth. I am guided by Spirit, not by expectation.

I am rich in faith, love, and wisdom. I live from abundance, not scarcity.

Just as someone who once had little learns to wear luxury with ease, I too release the old garments of self-doubt and step into the wardrobe of divine confidence. I no longer live by borrowed beliefs or secondhand ideas — I am clothed in originality, authenticity, and grace.

I see beyond appearances. I use the world as a canvas, but I never confuse it with my worth.

I am free to think, to create, to feel deeply, and to live boldly. I am ever-evolving, yet always aligned with the core of who I am

— God's reflection in motion.

Today, I move through life as my truest self — free, radiant, and divinely guided.

And so it is.

The Art of Being Her

An affirmation for confidence, individuality, and inner peace

I am one of a kind — a beautiful expression of something greater moving through me. There's a light within me that's always expanding, guiding me toward my next level.

I don't compare my path to anyone else's. I'm learning to honor my pace, my timing, and the way life unfolds for me. My uniqueness is my superpower.

Each day, I choose to be the best version of myself. I speak kindly to my reflection. I appreciate how far I've come and stay open to what's still becoming.

I give love freely. I attract peace easily. I show up fully as me. My thoughts shape my reality, so I fill my mind with things that make me feel whole, worthy, and alive.

Life supports me. The universe responds to my confidence.

I am healthy. I am happy. I am free.

Living in Fullness

My life is overflowing with goodness — not because everything is perfect, but because I've learned to see the beauty in every season. I am done living half-heartedly; I'm choosing fullness — full joy, full peace, full faith. I am open to receive everything God has written for me, and I believe I am worthy of abundance in every form. My spirit is rich, my mind is calm, and my heart is open. I don't chase what's mine; I attract it through gratitude and grace. I am living proof that when faith meets flow, fullness follows.

Her Higher Self Awakened

An affirmative prayer for renewal, clarity, and inner strength

Today I align my will with what is right and peaceful. I release the need to control, compare, or prove, and instead open myself to higher wisdom and balance.

My ego softens; my spirit expands. I am being renewed from within—clear-minded, centered, and in harmony with life.

I rise above small thinking and step fully into purpose. My energy is guided by love, and every choice I make is touched by grace.

The higher power within me—my truest self—moves through every detail of my life with calm precision. Everything unfolding for me is intentional, loving, and aligned.

I accept the strength, clarity, and peace that are already mine. I use my energy wisely: to build, to heal, to create, to love.

My life is my sanctuary—steady, illuminated, and filled with purpose.

I am renewed. I am guided. I am whole.

Her Power Within

An affirmative prayer for confidence, freedom, and divine flow

I am the creator of my own peace and the instigator of my good. Everything I need to live fully—joy, freedom, abundance, and love—is already within me.

Nothing outside of me defines my happiness. I decide what has power in my life, and today, I choose faith, purpose, and joy.

I release any belief that limits me. Every thought that once held me back dissolves in the light of awareness. I move freely, unbound by fear or doubt.

The energy that flows through the universe flows through me. I am aligned with a force greater than myself, one that responds to my belief and intention.

I think higher thoughts. I speak words of love and confidence. I act from peace, not pressure.

My good is already here—it's unfolding through every choice I make and every truth I embrace.

I am powerful, radiant, and in flow with divine abundance.

I am all that I desire to be.

Light Within Her

An affirmative prayer for peace, alignment, and divine order

The presence of God lives within me — steady, loving, and full of light. That power is infinite love, unshakable peace, and perfect joy flowing through every part of my being.

I am connected to divine goodness in all its forms. Everything unfolding in my life comes from that source of love, and everything is working for my highest good.

Even when things appear uncertain, I trust the outcome is still good because God is good. I call forth the blessings that already have my name on them.

Today, I align with a higher frequency. New ideas, new clarity, and new confidence find their way to me with ease. I attract what's meant for me — the right people, opportunities, and peace of mind.

At the center of my being is balance. There's a divine rhythm within me that knows exactly what to do and when to do it. Everything in my life is being brought into harmony, effortlessly and beautifully.

From this moment forward, I walk in calm assurance. My heart is light. My path is clear. My spirit is aligned.

And my life is a joyful reflection of divine order.

SECTION 6 : MOVED BY GRACE

Perfectly Her

An affirmative prayer for wholeness, peace, and divine alignment

Everything God creates is whole, complete, and without flaw — and that includes me. I release the need to fix, compare, or criticize. I am already becoming who I was designed to be.

The same divine order that holds the universe together is at work in me, through me, and around me. Every area of my life

— my health, my purpose, my ideas, my relationships — is unfolding in perfect timing and harmony.

I let go of the urge to look for what's wrong. I choose instead to see what's right. I see beauty where there once was doubt, peace where there once was pressure, and love where there once was fear.

My subconscious mind is cleared of every false story. I no longer speak from imperfection — I speak from truth.

God's love fills me, steadies me, and renews me. I walk in confidence knowing there is divine perfection within me and all around me.

I am aligned. I am whole. I am complete.

I live in the rhythm of perfect peace.

Guided by Grace

An affirmative prayer for trust, peace, and divine direction

I am a divine creation of God — fully seen, fully loved, and always guided. The same Spirit that created life itself is working through me, leading me toward everything meant for me.

Doors open with ease because nothing divinely aligned is ever closed to me. I move through life knowing that divine order is unfolding in every detail, in perfect timing.

I trust the plan even when I can't see every step. I relax into God's rhythm. I breathe in peace and exhale control.

Each day, I affirm that there is a right place and a right path designed just for me. I walk it with faith, not fear — with assurance, not anxiety.

God's love surrounds me. His presence sustains me. I am guided in every decision and protected in every moment. My mind is calm, my spirit is steady, and my body rests in divine balance.

I am aligned with purpose. I am sustained by peace. I am moved by grace.

In Tune With the Knower

An affirmative prayer for clarity, confidence, and divine rhythm

I move through this day in harmony with peace. My spirit is steady, my mind is clear, and my heart is open to divine wisdom. I am never without guidance — I carry it within me.

The voice inside me is calm and sure. It speaks through intuition, through timing, through the quiet knowing that I am where I need to be. I no longer rush or doubt. I listen, and I follow.

I honor the woman I'm becoming. I walk with assurance, not because I have every answer, but because I trust the One who leads me toward them.

Every experience brings growth. Every step reveals purpose. My confidence doesn't come from control — it comes from connection.

I am supported by divine order. I am aligned with peace, surrounded by love, and strengthened by grace.

Today, I walk with ease, led by wisdom deeper than thought — the quiet, faithful rhythm of the Knower within.

Moved by Grace

I move through life with ease because grace goes before me. I no longer strive or struggle — I flow. Every step I take is supported by something greater than me. Even when I can't see the full picture, I trust that the path is unfolding in divine order. Grace reminds me that I don't have to earn what's already mine. I release the pressure to be perfect and make peace with my becoming. Everything that's meant for me moves toward me with gentleness and clarity. I am guided, grounded, and growing in grace. Each moment is an opportunity to soften, to trust, and to let love lead the way.

Uninterrupted Flow

An affirmative prayer for peace, consistency, and divine momentum

Nothing can block what's meant for me. The same divine rhythm that keeps the world in motion moves through my life without pause. Every plan, every purpose, and every blessing unfolds in perfect order.

My thoughts rise above fear and limitation. I no longer live by appearances or temporary circumstances — I live by truth. The wisdom that created me continues to express through me, bringing new ideas, new opportunities, and new beginnings that never truly end.

I do not lose. I evolve. Every change, every shift, every closure is simply life redirecting me toward expansion.

There is no interruption in divine timing, no break in the flow of good. What is mine cannot be withheld, and what departs makes room for more.

I am a living part of divine order — steady, unbothered, and in motion.

Everything in my life is coming together beautifully. I am aligned with peace, and peace never pauses.

I flow forward in faith, untouched by interruption.

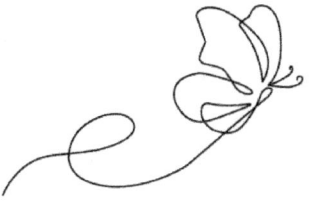

Mind of Clarity

An affirmative prayer for divine intelligence and inspired direction

My thoughts are clear, focused, and aligned with peace. I am connected to a higher wisdom that leads me with precision and grace. Every idea I need comes to me in the right moment, fully formed and ready to grow.

Confusion has no home in me. Indecision fades as I choose alignment over anxiety. I move with confidence, knowing that divine understanding guides every step I take.

I allow inspired ideas to flow through me easily. My thoughts are organized, my words are intentional, and my actions are led by purpose.

The same creative force that shapes galaxies is shaping my path — expanding my vision, refining my choices, and revealing the next right move.

Everything connected to my purpose flourishes. My work, my

ideas, and my opportunities are infused with excellence. I think clearly, love deeply, and act wisely.

I am one with divine intelligence. I am guided, aligned, and unstoppable.

Quiet Conversations

An affirmative prayer for connection, clarity, and inner peace

Today, I slow down and listen. I make space to hear the quiet guidance that lives within me — the calm voice that knows what I need before I even ask.

I feel deeply connected to the presence of God within and around me. That connection fills me with peace, confidence, and a sense of belonging. The more I tune inward, the easier it becomes to love, understand, and communicate with others.

In this stillness, I find clarity. The answers I've been reaching for start to rise naturally to the surface. I don't have to chase them

— I just have to be open enough to receive.

I trust the whispers of wisdom that come through prayer, silence, and reflection. Every time I listen, I am reminded that I am guided, supported, and never alone.

I am excited for what's unfolding. New ideas, new peace, and new opportunities are flowing toward me right now.

I am open. I am receptive. I am in harmony with life.

Thank you, God — for hearing me always, and for teaching me to listen.

The Presence That Heals Her

An affirmative prayer for women walking in renewal, peace, and divine confidence

In stillness, I feel God's presence resting within me — steady, loving, and gentle. His spirit fills the quiet spaces of my heart, reminding me that I am never forgotten, never unseen, and never without guidance.

The presence of God heals me — not just my body, but my emotions, my dreams, and the hidden corners of my heart. His love is the softest kind of strength, and it meets me exactly where I am.

Every part of my life is touched by divine order. God is at the center of my thoughts, my creativity, my relationships, and my work. His peace flows through my words, His wisdom directs my choices, and His grace goes before me in all things.

I let go of fear, comparison, and control. I no longer chase what's uncertain — I rest in what's already promised. God's timing is perfect, and His hand is steady on my path.

I am filled with renewed energy and inspiration. The same power that raised me through heartbreak, disappointment, and doubt is the same power that propels me toward healing, wholeness, and new beginnings.

I am a woman of vision, strength, and faith. I take bold steps, not because I have all the answers, but because I trust the One who does.

My life is not behind; it is unfolding. Every lesson, every pause, every redirection is proof of divine love at work.

I walk forward with softness and strength — radiant, confident, and covered in grace.

Everything concerning me is being healed, aligned, and made beautiful in God's perfect timing.

I am renewed. I am restored. I am her — whole, loved, and healed by His presence.

Power in Her Flow

An affirmative prayer for divine alignment, healing, and inner abundance

There is a loving, powerful presence moving through me right now. I don't have to force it, chase it, or earn it — I simply allow it. God's power flows through every part of my being, bringing peace to my spirit and order to my life.

This presence surrounds me wherever I go. It's the quiet strength that guides my thoughts, the calm that steadies my emotions, and the light that clears away anything not meant for me.

I am connected to something greater — a power that only knows love, health, and abundance. As I align with that power, everything in my life aligns with me.

I release tension, fear, and resistance. I choose to flow instead of fight. I let joy rise through me, peace fill me, and clarity lead me. Every thought I think invites healing, wholeness, and harmony.

Divine order is setting everything in its right place — in my
mind, my body, and my world.

I am open to new blessings, new ideas, and new levels of peace. I
believe that what's flowing toward me now is good, balanced,
and abundant.

I am centered. I am guided. I am in flow with divine love — and
everything in my life is coming into perfect alignment.

Flowing with Purpose

Purpose isn't something I chase — it's something I embody. I was designed with intention, and everything I've experienced is shaping me into who I'm meant to be. I flow with purpose because I know my life has meaning, even in the quiet seasons.

I trust that God placed me here on purpose and for a purpose. My gifts make room for me, and my presence carries impact. I no longer rush my path — I allow purpose to rise from within me naturally. Each day, I wake up with clarity, confidence, and calm, knowing that I am right where I'm supposed to be. I am walking in divine flow — radiant, aligned, and unstoppable.

SECTION 7: HEALED LOVE ERA

Guarded by Grace

An affirmative prayer for mindset, peace, and divine alignment

Today, I honor the power of my thoughts. I understand that what I choose to focus on becomes the energy that shapes my life. My mind is sacred space, and I protect it with peace.

I fill my thoughts with beauty, gratitude, and faith — and I see that same beauty reflected back to me in every part of my world.

I no longer force outcomes or try to fix everything around me. True change begins within, so I turn inward and align with calm confidence. From that place, everything else finds order.

I release the need to control others. My only responsibility is to stay true to my purpose, my peace, and my connection to God. Divine power moves through my thoughts, guiding me toward right action and peaceful solutions. I am supported by the same wisdom that sustains the universe — strong, steady, and unshakable.

Today, I think with clarity. I feel with faith. I move with grace. What I believe, I become. What I speak, I see. And what I give to God returns multiplied in love and good.

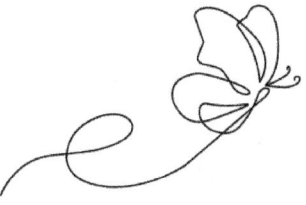

The Healing Within Her

An affirmative prayer for forgiveness, love, and divine renewal

The presence of God within me is alive and whole — a quiet strength that heals every space once touched by pain. His life moves through me, renewing my spirit, cleansing my thoughts, and restoring my heart to peace.

I am connected to divine love, and that love expands through me. It shows me how to release what no longer belongs, how to see people through grace, and how to meet myself with compassion.

I no longer carry resentment or old hurt. Every wound is a teacher, every memory a moment of growth. I forgive myself for what I didn't know and release others for what they couldn't give.

The spirit within me brings balance to my emotions and clarity to my heart. I am not defined by pain — I am shaped by healing.

Today, I think loving thoughts. I speak kind words. I make room for joy to return. God's peace is my protection, His grace my grounding, and His presence my constant renewal.

I am healed, forgiven, and free — filled with light, overflowing with love, and fully at peace.

Peace Lives Here Now

I've made peace my new home. I no longer chase closure or over- explain my heart — I choose serenity instead. What's behind me has served its purpose, and what's ahead of me is drenched in promise. I let calm settle where chaos used to live. My healed heart doesn't rush, compete, or cling — it simply rests. I trust that what's meant for me will arrive with ease and stay with grace. I am no longer at war with my past; I am in harmony with my present. Peace is not something I wait for — it's something I've become.

Wrapped in Love

An affirmative prayer for divine peace, safety, and self-acceptance

God's presence lives within me — quiet, steady, and sure. It fills every part of my being with warmth and light. I don't have to reach for it; I simply rest in it.

My entire life is surrounded and sustained by love. Every heartbeat, every breath, every thought is touched by this divine tenderness. Where love is, fear dissolves. Where love moves, healing happens.

I trust the love of God to renew everything that feels broken.

This love is patient, powerful, and limitless — nothing can stand against it.

Today, I choose to see myself through love's eyes. I honor the God-presence within me, and I extend that same grace to others. Every person I meet carries a spark of this same divine light.

Love restores what worry once fractured. It softens what pride once hardened. It fills every empty space with peace.

I am whole because love lives here.

Thank you, God, for this love that heals, restores, and completes me.

I receive it fully. I release it freely. And I let it be so.

All Things Bloom in Love

An affirmative prayer for softness, renewal, and divine purpose

Love is the rhythm of everything real. It's the quiet pulse behind creation, the gentle force that brings life into harmony. That same love moves through me—steady, endless, and full of grace.

I was made from love's intention, designed to express kindness, beauty, and strength. Every time I choose love—over fear, over pride, over pain—I return to who I truly am.

Love expands me. It teaches me to release what is heavy, to speak softly even when I'm healing loudly, and to believe that forgiveness doesn't make me weak—it makes me free.

Through love, I remember that I don't need to chase peace; it already lives within me. Love draws the right people, the right opportunities, and the right timing into my path.

My thoughts are lighter, my words gentler, my actions aligned. I am covered by something sacred, a presence that whispers, *"You are held. You are growing. You are enough."*

Today, I let love guide everything I do—how I listen, how I give, how I live.

I am becoming softer, stronger, and more whole, one act of love at a time.

Loved and Loving Again

I am no longer afraid to love or to be loved. Healing has softened me, not hardened me. My heart is open — not because it was never broken, but because it was beautifully rebuilt. I attract love that feels safe, reciprocal, and rooted in truth. I don't perform for love; I embody it. I am surrounded by relationships that honor my peace, celebrate my growth, and water my joy. I give and receive love freely, knowing that I am already complete. Love flows to me easily because I am aligned with the kind of love that comes from God — patient, kind, and real.

Love Lights My Way

An affirmative prayer for openness, connection, and divine compassion

Love is the heartbeat of creation — the quiet power that holds everything together. It lives within me, flows through me, and connects me to every living thing.

God's love is unconditional and ever-present. It doesn't ask for perfection; it simply asks me to receive it. No matter where I am in my journey, I am always held within love's embrace.

Today, I open my heart wider. I release the walls I've built from fear and disappointment, and I allow love to flow freely again — through my words, my thoughts, and my presence.

I see the light of God in others, even when it's hard to see. I choose compassion over judgment, and peace over pride. The more I love, the freer I become.

I let my actions reflect gratitude. I speak life, I give kindness, and I carry warmth wherever I go. Love transforms the spaces I enter and softens the hearts I meet.

My life shines brighter when love leads the way. Every moment becomes sacred when seen through love's eyes.

Today and always, I choose to live as love in motion — radiant, gentle, and full of grace.

My Healed Era Is Holy

This season of my life feels light, soft, and sacred. I'm no longer surviving — I'm thriving. I wake up each day knowing peace is my portion and joy is my birthright. Healing didn't make me hard; it made me whole. I'm proud of how far I've come and excited for what's ahead. Every lesson became a blessing, and every heartbreak made room for deeper love. I walk with grace, speak with tenderness, and live with faith that everything unfolding now is for my good. This is my healed, loved, and glowing era — and it only gets better from here.

SECTION 8: GRACE & GRATITUDE GLOW- UP

Grateful & Growing

An affirmative prayer for abundance, peace, and divine alignment

Today, I begin with thankfulness. I give thanks for the breath in my body, the beauty around me, and the lessons that continue to shape me. Gratitude connects me to God's presence—it reminds me that everything I have and everything I am is grace in motion.

I practice gratitude until it becomes my natural rhythm, my first response to life. Every thank you I whisper multiplies my blessings and expands my peace.

No matter what today brings, I choose to see good in it. Every challenge carries wisdom. Every delay hides divine timing.

Every ordinary moment is touched by purpose.

I am open to increase—spiritually, emotionally, and materially. My storehouse is within me, overflowing with ideas, creativity, and provision. Gratitude keeps it full; faith keeps it flowing.

I thank God for the love in my life, for clarity in my steps, for the quiet ways He shows up daily.

My heart is light, my hands are open, and my life is abundant.

I give thanks, and it returns multiplied.

Full of Wonder

An affirmative prayer for gratitude, curiosity, and divine joy

Today, I wake up in awe of life. Every breath, every sunrise, every tiny detail feels like a love note from God reminding me how extraordinary it is to simply exist.

I let go of the need to control or understand everything. Instead, I choose to marvel — at the timing, at the lessons, at the beauty that unfolds even in uncertainty.

My spirit is wide open to wonder. I walk through this day expecting goodness, expecting joy, expecting divine surprises that make me smile and remind me I'm cared for.

Wisdom lives within me, quietly guiding each step. The same power that spins the stars is the same power shaping my story.

I trust that, and I'm grateful for it.

I thank God for the people who walk beside me — for friendships that feel like light, for love that refills my soul, and for connection that reminds me I'm never alone.

Gratitude is my strength and my glow. The more I notice beauty, the more beauty finds me. The more I bless, the more blessings multiply.

Today, I live like everything is a miracle — because it is.

Grace Made Room for Me

I am walking through doors that grace opened. Every opportunity that finds me is proof that I'm in alignment with God's timing. I don't have to chase what's mine — I just have to stay ready. I am grateful for the seasons that stretched me, because they prepared me for this one. I thank God for the open doors, the quiet yeses, and even the divine delays that taught me patience. I am where I'm supposed to be, doing what I'm meant to do, and grace made it all possible.

Perfect by Design

An affirmative prayer for gratitude, faith, and divine alignment

Everything in creation carries God's touch of perfection — and that includes me. I was designed with purpose, shaped by love, and guided by wisdom that knows no mistakes.

Today, I trust the divine intelligence within me. It whispers when to pause, when to act, and when to simply believe. My faith is not passive — it's movement, energy, and alignment in action.

I move forward with grace, confident that every step I take is supported by a power greater than I can see. Even when things appear uncertain, I know beauty is unfolding beneath the surface.

I choose to see people and situations through the lens of love.

Every encounter becomes an opportunity to see God's goodness in disguise.

I am thankful for the clarity that grows from faith, for the health that flows through me, and for the abundance that constantly surrounds me.

Gratitude lifts my vision. Faith steadies my heart. Love keeps me centered.

I am whole, complete, and perfectly aligned with divine order. Today, I walk in peace — knowing I was never anything less than perfect by design.

Thank You in Advance

An affirmative prayer for gratitude, flow, and divine fullness

There's a power moving through my life that only knows good

— a steady, loving energy that keeps everything in motion. I
don't have to chase it; I just have to stay open to it.

Today, I live in thankfulness. Not just for what I see, but for
what's still becoming. Gratitude isn't something I practice
occasionally — it's how I breathe.

I give thanks for beauty I haven't yet noticed, for opportunities
that are already forming, and for every unseen blessing working
in my favor.

My thankfulness shifts my focus from lack to love, from waiting
to receiving. Each moment is a chance to witness how deeply
God cares for me.

I am grateful for the clarity that comes through peace, for the
lessons that shaped my wisdom, and for the gentle ways life
continues to reveal purpose.

My heart overflows, and everything I touch multiplies in grace.

Gratitude keeps me grounded in faith and lifted in joy.

Today, I say "thank you" — not because everything is perfect,
but because everything is purposeful.

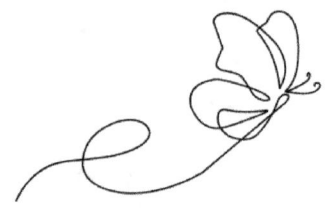

Thank You for the Becoming

I thank God not just for what I have, but for who I'm becoming.
Every challenge built character. Every blessing built faith. I'm
grateful for the lessons that didn't make sense until they bloomed
into favor. I live with a thankful heart — one that recognizes that
grace has always been covering me, even when I didn't see it.
Gratitude keeps me grounded; grace keeps me glowing. Every
breath, every opportunity, every connection is divine.

The Joy of Thank You

An affirmative prayer for expansion, joy, and divine overflow

Today, my heart feels wide open. Gratitude flows through me like sunlight, filling every corner of my life with warmth, joy, and possibility.

I give thanks for the power of life within me — the energy that creates, expands, and multiplies good in ways I can't always see. Gratitude opens doors I didn't even know were there.

I praise the Spirit that breathes through all things, the wisdom that guides me, and the love of God that keeps proving everything is possible.

I see beauty everywhere — in the sky that stretches endlessly, in the laughter of friends, in quiet mornings and bright new chances. My spirit celebrates all that's alive, all that's growing, and all that's becoming.

I'm grateful not just for my own blessings, but for the blessings of others — because when one heart expands, we all rise.

Today, I choose to walk in an attitude of joy and gratitude. I thank God for the abundance I already hold, and for the overflow that's still on its way.

Gratitude is my posture, joy is my rhythm, and praise is my power.

Everything in my life multiplies in grace — because I live in a constant "thank you."

Opportunities Find Me Easily

I am in a season where favor follows me. I thank God in advance for the doors that are already opening and the opportunities being prepared in my name. I walk with confidence knowing that every space I enter is blessed because I bring light with me. I attract divine connections, creative ideas, and aligned opportunities with ease. My gratitude magnetizes miracles — and grace ensures they arrive right on time.

This Moment Glows

An affirmative prayer for presence, joy, and divine awareness

Right here, in this breath, life is happening — vivid, sacred, and new. I let go of yesterday and stop reaching for tomorrow. I live this moment fully, and I recognize it as a miracle in motion.

The same Spirit that shaped the stars is alive within me, guiding my heartbeat, fueling my joy, and filling me with purpose. I don't need to chase meaning — I am already part of it.

I pause to feel sunlight on my skin, to hear laughter, to notice the beauty that hides in ordinary places. I see the world again for the first time — fresh, alive, and full of wonder.

I look at the people I love and feel deep gratitude that I get to share this moment with them. Every connection, every lesson, every breath is a reflection of divine love expressing itself through life.

Today, I choose awareness over distraction. I choose gratitude over hurry. I choose joy over fear.

This is the moment I've been waiting for — the one that reminds me I'm alive, whole, and surrounded by grace.

I receive it fully. I rejoice in it completely.

Grace in Every Yes

I thank God for every "yes" that stretched me and every "no" that redirected me. I see now that even closed doors were blessings in disguise. Grace covered me through it all. I'm grateful for new beginnings, fresh starts, and second chances. I no longer rush divine timing — I rest in it. Today, I move with gratitude, speak with faith, and glow in grace. I am living proof that what's meant for me will always find me.

SECTION 9: FRESH STARTS & SOFT GRACE

Right Now, I Rise

An affirmative prayer for renewal, expansion, and divine confidence

Right now, something within me is awakening. I feel lighter, softer, and stronger all at once. God's presence fills me — mind, body, and spirit — and I step fully into a new beginning.

Every cell in my body vibrates with new life. Every thought aligns with peace and purpose. I no longer shrink to fit old versions of myself. I expand boldly into the woman I was created to be.

I release every belief that limits me — fear, doubt, comparison, or lack. They no longer have a home here. My supply is infinite, my wisdom is divine, my opportunities are limitless, and my worth is already settled.

I am no longer bound by time or circumstance. The same God who made the stars breathes new possibilities into my path. This is my transformation. This is my moment of becoming. I am open to all the beauty and abundance that are already waiting for me.

Right now, I choose faith over fear, growth over comfort, and joy over hesitation.

Something wonderful is unfolding — in my spirit, in my story, and in every detail of my life.

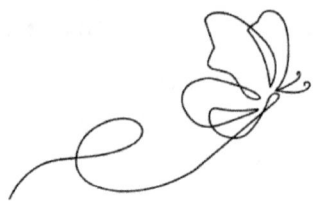

Brand-New Me

An affirmative prayer for renewal, confidence, and divine flow

God's presence fills me from the inside out — calm, powerful, and alive. When I quiet my thoughts, I can feel divine energy moving through me, restoring balance and awakening fresh inspiration.

I declare that my life is new. Every breath holds potential. Every moment is an open door waiting for faith to walk through.

I release the old with love — old fears, old patterns, old stories that no longer serve who I'm becoming. The past can't touch me because grace already rewrote my future.

Today, I choose the present — the only place where miracles happen. I build from a place of peace, creating my next chapter with thoughts rooted in purpose and power.

God supports my every move. Spirit gives me the ideas, vision, and courage to design a life filled with joy, beauty, and divine abundance.

I am open to a new day, a new energy, a new way of seeing life.

I live in harmony with divine wisdom and love, moving confidently toward everything that's meant for me.

This is my renewal. This is my becoming.

I am alive, aligned, and ready for what's next.

Becoming More

An affirmative prayer for courage, creativity, and divine expansion

God is still creating—and I am part of that creation. Every breath, every idea, every moment is proof that life is still unfolding through me.

I no longer fear what's new. I welcome it. Each sunrise holds a story I haven't lived yet, and I step into it with an open heart and a curious mind.

I dare to dream differently, to think beyond what I've known, and to believe that growth can feel both exciting and graceful. I am guided by Spirit into spaces that stretch me, not to break me—but to build me.

I let wonder lead me. I see beauty in the smallest things, and I let gratitude turn every ordinary day into something sacred.

The creative power of God expresses through me, turning fresh ideas into reality and faith into action.

I am not who I was yesterday—and that's the point. Each day I rise a little higher, think a little freer, and love a little deeper.

I am becoming more—beautifully, boldly, and by divine design.

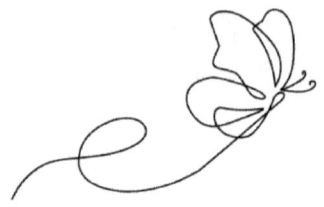

Grace for My Becoming

I give myself permission to start again — not from fear, but from
faith. I release the pressure to be perfect and make room for
peace instead. I am no longer defined by what I've outgrown.
Every ending was simply grace in disguise, guiding me back to
alignment.

Today, I choose to see myself through God's eyes — loved,
capable, and covered. I don't rush my becoming; I trust it. I move
at the pace of peace, knowing that soft progress is still progress.
My story is unfolding beautifully, and this new beginning is
proof that I am never too late, too lost, or too far gone to bloom
again.

Blooming Right Now

An affirmative prayer for renewal, awareness, and divine awakening

There is a sacred energy moving through me — soft but powerful, gentle yet unstoppable. God's love fills every corner of my being, restoring balance, peace, and beauty to my soul. I am fully alive in this moment. Each breath awakens new light within me. I am not waiting for a new season — I am the new season. The Spirit of renewal is alive in me right now.

I release what was and rise into what's next. My heart is open to divine rhythm, my mind clear with purpose, and my life blooming with fresh grace.

Just like flowers turn toward the sun, I turn toward God's light and feel myself growing — in wisdom, in faith, in love. The seeds I've planted are already taking root; something beautiful is unfolding through me.

Infinite goodness flows into every area of my life — new ideas, new peace, new joy, new abundance. I am supported by the same divine presence that holds the universe together.

This moment is sacred, full of promise and alive with possibility. I stand in awe of what God is creating through me right now.

I bloom in love, gratitude, and divine alignment.

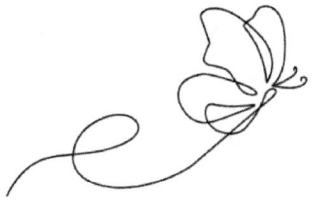

Made New Again

An affirmative prayer for fresh starts, soft faith, and divine alignment

Today, I release what no longer fits and make space for what's meant for me. New ideas, new joy, new peace, and new opportunities are flowing my way — all guided by God's perfect timing.

I am awakening to the presence of something greater within me

— the quiet, steady love of God that renews my spirit from the inside out. Each new beginning is a reminder that I am still becoming, still growing, still unfolding into the woman God envisioned.

I meet every moment with grace and gratitude. I no longer resist change — I welcome it. Every shift brings a lesson, every challenge reveals new strength, and every blessing reminds me that I am deeply favored.

My life is a reflection of divine renewal. God's light moves through me, refreshing my heart, restoring my purpose, and filling my path with peace.

I am the embodiment of newness — not because I've changed everything, but because I've learned to see everything through love.

What's ahead of me is greater than what's behind. I am made new, again and again, by grace.

Blossoming in New Light

I am entering a new season with a clear heart and a calm mind. The past no longer holds power over me — I've learned, I've healed, and I've outgrown what dimmed my light. Fresh starts feel good on me because I know they come with divine purpose.

I welcome every new opportunity, conversation, and connection with gratitude. I'm aligned with favor and guided by grace. I trust that God is already ahead of me, arranging everything for my good. I don't have to force what's flowing — I simply allow.

This is my season of softness, expansion, and divine renewal. I am ready for the beauty that's becoming me.

Rise in the Now

An affirmative prayer for renewal, courage, and divine becoming

Today, I release what was and rise fully into what is. Yesterday has served its purpose, and tomorrow will take care of itself — but right now, this moment, is sacred.

I no longer carry the weight of old stories, regrets, or versions of me that no longer fit. I lay them down gently and walk away in peace. Growth doesn't scare me anymore — I am ready for the new.

I feel God's spirit breathing new energy into every part of my life. Possibility flows through me. Purpose surrounds me. I am being renewed in real time.

I rise like light breaking through clouds — soft, radiant, and full of hope. What once limited me has lost its hold. I am stretching into new thoughts, new strength, and new awareness.

The Spirit within delights in my becoming. It moves through me, creating fresh ideas, fresh opportunities, and fresh grace.

I trust this process. I trust the timing. I trust myself.

This is my now — and in this now, I rise.

Greater Awakenings

An affirmative prayer for clarity, alignment, and divine flow

There's a powerful energy moving through me — one that clears out what's no longer aligned and makes space for everything meant for me.

I am open to divine flow. The same Spirit that orders the stars and holds the oceans steady is guiding my thoughts, my timing, and my next move. I trust this inner wisdom to lead me exactly where I'm supposed to be.

Love is the current that connects it all. It gathers the pieces of my life into balance and beauty. I let go of anything that limits me and make room for greater things — greater peace, greater purpose, greater grace.

Every outdated story, fear, or belief that once held me back is released. I declare it complete. What's leaving creates room for what's rising.

God's power within me is active, alive, and creating something beautiful through me right now. I feel it in my thoughts, my spirit, my emotions — a steady renewal that lifts me higher. Today, I say yes to growth, yes to love, yes to divine order. I move with the rhythm of grace, certain that every step is part of my becoming.

I am aligned, expanding, and fully open to all that God has prepared for me.

Becoming Brand New

An affirmative prayer for expansion, *self-belief, and divine confidence*

There is one divine wisdom flowing through all things — and that wisdom lives in me. God's mind and mine are connected, creating new pathways, new clarity, and new beginnings that reflect who I'm becoming.

I am no longer who I was yesterday. Each sunrise brings fresh opportunities to see myself as God sees me — whole, capable, radiant, and full of promise. My thoughts are creative, and my faith gives them form.

I speak life into my future. I affirm abundance, joy, and purpose in everything I touch. I don't wait for doors to open — I align with grace and watch them swing wide for me.

Every experience is shaping me into a wiser, softer, more powerful version of myself. I am constantly evolving, constantly expanding into the woman I was always meant to be.

I move with gratitude for where I am and excitement for what's next. My path is clear, my spirit is ready, and my good is already here.

I am becoming brand new — not by force, but by faith.

Bloom Gently

A prayer for the woman starting over and learning to give herself grace

God, thank You for the gift of new beginnings — for reminding me that even after the hardest seasons, life still finds ways to bloom.

Today, I release the pressure to have it all figured out. I let go of timelines, comparison, and the idea that I'm behind. I'm not late

— I'm aligned.

I trust that You are guiding my steps, even when the path feels unclear. I give myself permission to grow slowly, softly, and beautifully.

My journey doesn't have to be perfect to be purposeful. Every sunrise reminds me that grace resets everything — my spirit, my focus, my faith.

I am allowed to start over. I am allowed to begin again with peace. I am allowed to evolve into the woman You already see me as.

I walk into this new chapter open, unhurried, and unafraid —
because I know You're in every detail of my becoming.

Amen.

Fresh Grace, New Glow

A prayer for the girl finding faith again after feeling lost

Every morning I wake up, You remind me — I still have purpose, even when I've wandered. I still have beauty, even when I've broken. I still have You, and that's more than enough.

Today, I choose to see myself through Your eyes — loved, worthy, and capable of beginning again. I silence the voice that says I've failed and listen instead to the whisper that says, "You're safe to start anew."

I release shame and invite softness. I let go of striving and reach for surrender. I make peace with where I am and give thanks for how far I've come.

My new beginning doesn't have to be loud — it just has to be honest.

I trust that every ending carried me closer to grace, and every fresh start carries me closer to You.

I move forward with faith, covered in peace, glowing from the inside out.

Amen.

SECTION 10: "LIFE KEEPS POURING MORE GLOW, MORE GRACE, AND MORE GOODNESS MY WAY."

Soft Overflow

An affirmative prayer for divine provision, peace, and grace

Everything I need is already flowing toward me. My life is connected to an endless source — a divine river that never runs dry. I don't chase what's meant for me; I attract it through faith, gratitude, and trust.

God's love fills my life with ease. My needs are met before I even speak them, and my blessings arrive right on time. I am covered — emotionally, financially, spiritually, and creatively.

I don't have to cling or compete. My supply is steady, my mind is calm, and my heart is open to receive more good than I could ever imagine. I live in a constant rhythm of giving and receiving, flowing with divine order.

Today, I am rich in peace, love, and inspired ideas. My relationships are balanced and fulfilling. My spirit is full, my purpose is clear, and my life is blooming in divine timing. Every good thing with my name on it finds me easily. I am provided for, protected, and overflowing with grace.

Gratitude is my lifestyle. Overflow is my normal.

Becoming My Next Level

An affirmative prayer for growth, gratitude, and divine alignment

I am connected to divine wisdom — the same power that opens doors, expands dreams, and breathes life into new beginnings. God's thoughts toward me are good, and I align myself with that goodness right now.

I see myself clearly — confident, creative, and whole. Every day reveals more of who I truly am: loved, guided, and filled with purpose. I'm not waiting for a new chapter; I'm already living it.

I am the designer of my experience, co-creating with God. My thoughts are powerful, my energy magnetic, and my faith unshakable. What I imagine with love takes form in my reality with ease.

Each day, I am evolving — becoming softer in spirit, stronger in faith, and more open to divine opportunity. Growth feels good to me because I know it's guided.

New doors are opening effortlessly. Fresh ideas flow freely. My world expands beautifully, all in divine order.

I move forward with gratitude, grounded in peace, knowing that everything good is already mine — right here, right now.

This is my becoming. And it is blessed.

The Soft Power of Becoming

"I no longer rush my becoming. I no longer force what needs time to unfold. I am learning to trust the quiet, the still, the subtle shifts within me. I no longer chase proof of my growth — I feel it. I carry a soft power that doesn't demand to be seen to be real. I release the pressure to bloom on anyone else's timeline. I honor the small victories, the private healing, the quiet revolutions happening in my soul. Becoming is not a performance. It's a return to truth. And I am becoming more myself every day, gently, deeply, and without apology."

A Life That Blossoms

An affirmative prayer for expansion, faith, and divine fulfillment

I am no longer just existing — I am *becoming*. Each day is an invitation to rise higher, think deeper, and live fuller. I let go of survival mode and step boldly into the soft, steady rhythm of purpose.

My thoughts are fertile ground for miracles. What I plant with faith, I will see bloom in beauty. God's wisdom flows through my mind, guiding my choices, shaping my vision, and expanding my world.

I move with joy and expectation. Every new idea is a seed of divine possibility, already rooted in favor. I trust the process — knowing that everything meant for me is already unfolding.

Abundance surrounds me in every form: love that sustains me, opportunities that stretch me, and peace that keeps me steady. My life overflows with creative energy. I am free from limitation, open to transformation, and aligned with God's perfect plan.

This season is one of full bloom — not by chance, but by divine design.

I walk in new awareness: of peace, of purpose, of power, and of God's presence in every detail of my becoming.

Planted for Promise

An affirmative prayer for expansion, prosperity, and divine renewal

I'm no longer just going through life — I'm *growing* through it. Every thought I choose becomes a seed, and today, I plant them with intention, love, and faith.

The days of small thinking and survival are behind me. I move with vision, aligned with the limitless wisdom of God within me.

My thoughts rise higher, and my experiences follow. Faith opens every door meant for me.

I am surrounded by divine possibility — endless paths to peace, prosperity, and purpose. I don't chase what's mine; I nurture it, trust it, and allow it to bloom in divine timing. My ideas are fertile. My heart is open. My steps are guided.

I live from abundance, not lack. The same God who formed the stars supplies every need in my life. There is no shortage of good

— only the flow I allow myself to receive.

Health is within me. Joy is within me. Creativity, confidence, and divine favor are all within me. Every good thing is already mine; I simply rise to meet it.

My life overflows with beauty, provision, and peace. I honor what's growing and give thanks for what's on the way.

Today, I remember: I am planted for promise — watered by grace, and destined to bloom.

Power in My Peace

An affirmative prayer for divine energy, balance, and alignment

There's a power within me that's stronger than anything around me — steady, radiant, and unstoppable. It's the Spirit of God flowing through my life, guiding my steps, and anchoring my peace.

No matter what the world looks like, I remain grounded in calm confidence. My spirit doesn't waver with circumstances; it leads them. I am surrounded by divine energy that attracts clarity, favor, and alignment in all things.

I release every trace of worry, fear, or tension. I refuse to block my blessings with doubt. Instead, I breathe deeply and make room for God's flow to move freely through me — restoring balance, renewing strength, and revealing solutions.

The presence within me is powerful and peaceful all at once. It gives life to my ideas, harmony to my relationships, and direction to my dreams. Every word I speak carries creative energy; every choice I make sends goodness into motion.

I am in sync with the rhythm of divine order. Peace fuels my productivity, and joy amplifies my results. I move with ease, trust, and quiet power.

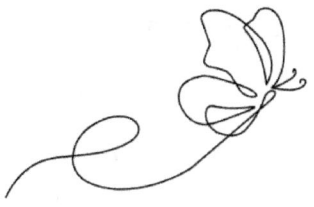

The Joy That Lives in Me

An affirmative prayer for happiness, confidence, and divine freedom

God delights in my joy — it's part of how His light shines through me. Happiness isn't something I chase; it's something that rises naturally from within me.

I was created to live in fullness — to love freely, to laugh loudly, and to express the creative spark that makes me unique. Joy is my natural state, my spiritual signature, the rhythm of my life. Today, I choose to feel good on purpose. I release the need to wait for the "right" moment to be happy — this moment is enough. I am enough. The joy within me is a well that never runs dry.

My energy is magnetic. My smile carries healing. My confidence radiates peace. I see the beauty in my own becoming, and I celebrate it.

Joy flows through every part of me — through my work, my words, my connections, my dreams. It reminds me that I am fully alive, fully loved, and fully free.

I walk in lightness. I live in laughter. I breathe in gratitude. I embody the joy of divine creation.

Today, I don't just feel joy — I *am* joy.

Spirit Within Me

An affirmative prayer for inner peace, divine love, and daily renewal

Each day, the Spirit within me wakes up ready to love, create, and shine. God's presence fills every breath, every thought, and every heartbeat. I don't have to search for peace — it already lives in me.

When I center my thoughts on divine love, I feel everything shift. Peace softens my mind. Joy steadies my emotions. I am reminded that I am never separate from the Source that made me.

God's love is not distant — it's alive, moving through every part of me. It restores what's tired, quiets what's restless, and renews my strength from the inside out.

I carry this love into everything I do. It guides how I speak, how I show up, how I respond to the world around me. Wherever I go, peace follows.

The Spirit of joy walks with me today. It lifts my energy, aligns my intentions, and fills me with lightness. I start this day openhearted — ready to love, ready to grow, ready to be used for good.

God's presence in me is my calm, my creativity, and my confidence.

I am alive with divine purpose — and I move through this day in peace.

Peace in My Progress

I am proud of how far I've come, even when the steps were small. Progress doesn't always have to be loud — sometimes it looks like peace. I celebrate every moment I chose grace over pressure, faith over fear, and love over doubt. I trust that the seeds I've planted are growing, even in silence. I walk like I already have what I've prayed for because I know my next level is unfolding in perfect rhythm with God's will.

Glow in His Grace

A prayer for the girl learning to trust the timing

Life keeps pouring more glow, more grace, and more goodness my way — even when I can't see it yet.

I release the need to rush what God is still writing. Every delay is divine direction. Every closed door is protection.

Today, I choose calm over control. I choose faith over fear. I let grace hold me where striving once did.

God's favor surrounds me like light — soft, steady, and undeniable.

My peace multiplies. My blessings unfold naturally.

I don't chase what's already mine. I attract it by being aligned, grateful, and radiant.

I am walking in grace, glowing in peace, and trusting that what's meant for me will never miss me.

Soft Life, Strong Faith

A prayer for the woman who's done forcing and started flowing

I was never meant to carry everything — just the confidence that God's already working it out.

So today, I release the heavy and pick up the holy. I breathe deeper. I smile easier. I walk softer.

God's hand is in every detail — from my rest to my rise, from my prayers to my purpose.

Abundance flows to me because I trust that I am taken care of. Peace is my posture. Ease is my evidence.

I let life love me back. I glow because grace guides me. I win by

staying soft.

Becoming Her, Becoming Still

I no longer rush my rise. My next level doesn't demand stress —
it requires stillness. I am at peace with where I am because I
know God is already preparing what's next. I release the need to
prove and rest in divine timing. My growth is graceful, my glow
is genuine, and my purpose unfolds with ease. I am aligned, I am
evolving, and I am becoming everything I once prayed for —
calmly, confidently, and completely.

Everything Good Finds Me

A prayer for faith, flow, and divine overflow

God keeps surprising me — not with chaos, but with calm. Not with stress, but with sweetness.

I'm learning that when I surrender, I receive. When I stop doubting, I start blooming.

Every blessing that belongs to me is already on its way, perfectly timed and beautifully wrapped in grace.

My joy attracts more joy. My faith multiplies my favor. My gratitude opens new doors daily.

I'm surrounded by divine goodness — peace in my mornings, beauty in my moments, and abundance in my days.

Life keeps pouring more glow, more grace, and more goodness my way — and I'm finally soft enough to receive it.

Thank You

To every woman who picked up this book—thank you.

Thank you for choosing yourself.

For speaking life over your journey.

For daring to affirm your worth, your healing, your purpose, and your power.

This book was made for you, but more importantly, it was made *from* you—your resilience, your softness, your strength, your becoming.

Whether you whispered these affirmations in quiet moments or declared them boldly to the sky, know this: every word planted something powerful in you.

Keep affirming her. Keep showing up.

You are seen, you are sacred, and you are just getting started.

With love and power,

Jaylin Gibson

First printing: 11/25

ISBN: 979-8-9937322-4-4

Published by: Champagne and Chandeliers LLC

www.ingramcontent.com/pod-product-compliance
Lightning Source LLC
Chambersburg PA
CBHW060418130626
46555CB00005B/2118